Mothering Matters

By Melanie Hewitt

First Edition. Published and printed in the United States.

Printed by Lulu.com.

In memory of my mother, Shirley Ann Lenz Brown,
with thanks for my life and for all her known and
unknown acts of love.

To Carly and Alyssa, who have brought me immense
joy and have given me the gift of mothering two
thoughtful, creative and beautiful souls.

And to my Jerry, whose sustaining love, encouragement
and wise perspective has allowed me to enjoy
an incredibly fulfilling life – my
love and gratitude forever.

Chapter One

THE POWER OF MOTHERS

I am older than my mother. That may seem impossible, but it's true. My mom died when she was only forty-seven and she will always remain that age in my mind. I am now over fifty and it surprises me at times when the face I see in the mirror looks older than my memory of hers.

I still miss my mom immensely. In the years following her death as I completed college, got married, started a career, faced a challenging trial with infertility and became a mother to twin daughters, I didn't have my mother to guide me through any of it. I realized through her absence and my grief in losing her what a vital role a mother plays in the lives of her children.

I owe my life to my mother. You owe your life to yours. This is not news. If not for mothers, not a single person would have walked this earth.   In all of human history these women have been a critical part. They are essential players in the great play, yet most of the time they are not even mentioned. It is as if all the notable men and women through the ages sprang unaided and fully formed from the earth. Though history may not mention them, individuals are often aware of the great debt owed to their mother. Abraham Lincoln acknowledged his with the words "All that I am, or hope to be, I owe to my angel mother."

My mother was a powerful force in shaping my life. I know that I have been that force in the lives of my daughters. Mothers nurture and teach, guide and sustain the children they have borne. It is their voice that is most clearly heard in the formative years; they are the power behind the throne. They have significant influence on the character and outlook of their children. Mothers are owed a huge debt and hold great power in their hands, yet they are not always recognized for their contributions.

It is an inescapable fact that we humans require the DNA from a mother and a father to exist. In addition to the basic building blocks of life that she provides, however, a mother also is the vehicle by which that life is nurtured, in which it grows, and from which it enters into the world. She is the single most important factor in her child's initial survival. Through the raising of their children, mothers help determine what the future holds for our world. There is a power and a glory to mothering. It is a high calling.

Mothers matter! When mothering is done well, the whole world benefits; when it is done poorly, the whole world suffers.

Mother

She is Nature

She is Earth

Vast and powerful

Yet intimately tender

She nurtures and sustains

In her waters is Life

On her breath all growth depends

Vital and creative

She channels the Divine

She is

Mother

Chapter Two

GOODBYE

Mom was diagnosed with non-Hodgkin's lymphoma in 1982 as I was finishing my freshman year of college. Through the first rounds of chemotherapy she stayed strong and positive, never complaining, just getting a wig and scarves to cover her head and continuing to work on her many projects as she could. A few months later our parents called a family meeting. The seven of us siblings, ranging in age from nine to twenty-three, sat around our small living room floor as they sat on the couch. We had never done this before and I knew something serious was going on. I sat close to my youngest sister, Megan. One of my brothers threw a blanket over his head to try to separate himself from what was happening.

Mom told us then that more tumors had grown.

"I want you all to know that I have to have surgery this time and..." her voice broke and she paused. "I don't think I can survive it. I am so weak still from the chemo treatments. I wanted you to be ready for that possibility."

Stunned, tears filled my eyes and I was unable to talk. I put my arm around my little sister. There was a heavy silence in the room.

Finally my older sister, Maureen, spoke up.

"Mom, you know we all love you very much. We will help you through this."

Life took a sharp turn at that point. I had to confront the very real possibility that my mom might die. Saying good bye to her as she was wheeled into that surgery was one of the hardest moments of my life. Praying in the small hospital chapel while her life hung in the balance, I knew I might never talk with her again. She made it through the surgery, with all her strength and toughness, and was able to return home a few days later.

When I went back to college, shortly after, life fell into a new kind of pattern. Though outwardly all was oddly normal, there was an unease that permeated everything. In May of 1983 as I finished my sophomore year of college, Mom chose to undergo an experimental autologous bone marrow transplant procedure as tumors continued to appear and grow.

She endured powerful radiation and chemotherapy treatments to try to kill off the cancer cells, hoping that she could recover when her own bone marrow was then reintroduced.

The toll taken on her body by the treatments was tremendous and her kidneys were failing. I was there with my dad in the hospital, helping care for her. My siblings and I had decorated her hospital room with a large poster covered with pictures of her seven children, our attempt to let her know we were with her every day, though she was many miles away from home. I sat with her and tried to do the little things that would make her more comfortable, getting her ice water, balm for her severely chapped lips and gently rubbing her back to ease her stiffness.

My older brother, Tim, was there the day the doctors told us her kidneys had failed and she would have to undergo dialysis to try to save her life. Mom could hardly speak, as the chemotherapy had caused terrible sores in her mouth, yet she spoke aloud every word of the Lord's Prayer as we all joined in, gathered around her there in her bed. Tim bore me up with his arm around my shoulders as we prayed.

They wheeled her down to the Intensive Care Unit and I took the first shift of sitting with her there. Through the cold rails of her bed, I held her hand.

"You are doing great, Mom. Keep fighting." I told her often as she struggled through the night. "I love you."

The monitors with their blue lights blinking and the beeps and alarms from the machines attached to her kept me alert, though she seemed to sleep off and on.

At four in the morning, my dad came in to relieve me and told me to go get some sleep in mom's old hospital room. My mother, exhausted and barely able to speak, said

"No! She won't get any sleep there." Then, addressing me, "Go back to the dorm room so you can rest."

And so I did as my mom said and walked across the street in the dark of the night to the sparse dorm room where Dad and I had been staying.

It was the last mothering I would ever receive from her. She died four hours later with my dad by her side, holding her hand.

The Last Hug

As I took my leave that day
the possibilities were known.
Time could be short,
further meetings in doubt.
My mother hugged me,
in itself a rare thing,
and I hugged tightly back;
a lasting gift to one another
in that fragile moment.
In the emptiness after
her death
I awoke from a dream
vividly clear.
Lingering in my senses
her presence remained
with arms around me
giving one last hug.

Chapter Three

REMEMBERING

I wish you could have known my mother. I wish I could have known her better. One of my greatest sorrows is that I do not have many clear memories of her from my childhood. She is always there, just not in full focus. We tend to remember the unusual and the extraordinary things from our past. My mother was an ordinary, everyday presence and so her actions are not ingrained in my memory.

One thing I do remember about Mom is her strength. Though fairly small of stature, I thought my mom was the strongest woman in the world. She could open any jar, no matter how stuck the lid was, and she was able to lift heavy furniture without any apparent difficulty. Not only was she strong physically, but morally, as well. Her actions, including sending her children to inner city schools to create her own desegregation plan, working in and having her children attend low income pre-schools, and serving on innumerable committees to improve educational offerings in all schools, instilled in me an inner moral compass which guides me to this day. She lived out her principles with honesty and integrity.

She was a remarkable woman, and I'm sure I don't fully appreciate all of her many talents and gifts. I wish that I knew more of her thoughts and dreams, too. It hurts that I will never be able to ask her the things I'd like to know about her.

Born on an Iowa farm in 1935, the fourth of six children, my mother, Shirley Ann Lenz, graduated as valedictorian of her high school class in Mount Vernon, Iowa and received a nursing degree from the University of Iowa in 1958.

Her own mother died while Shirley was in college. She never spoke to us of this loss and I always wondered how she coped with it. Mom was very contained, not emotional like me, and even when I questioned her, she never shared anything about her mother or her feelings when she died. She kept those things private and I realize in retrospect that she never talked to me about emotions and feelings. She kept her sorrows to herself.

Though her life followed the script of many women of her era (married after college to Donald J. Brown, not employed outside the home after her first child was born) she was an advocate for social change. I know now, reading the tributes from her friends and colleagues we received after her death, that she was ahead of her time in many ways. She advocated for women's rights and civil rights in a time when that was not a popular thing to do.

Our dining room table was often covered with flyers and we would be enlisted to help her fold, label and stamp them to be mailed out in support of one or another of her causes. She worked tirelessly for education issues, early childhood affordable quality care, natural childbirth education, refugee support and served on many community boards and school committees, yet her primary energies were given to her family.

My mom sat in the stands for countless hours for her kids. She supported all of our activities, becoming a gymnastics judge when there were not enough in the area and enthusiastically working for the swim teams we joined. She provided a stable, loving home and she encouraged and sometimes challenged each of us to be our best in whatever we were passionate about. She was strict with TV access and curfews, hard on us if we showed bad attitudes and had a high standard for behavior. But as I grew older, I realized how lucky I was to have a mother like her. It is because of her love and care that I have this life. I thank her often in my mind as I face the day to day decisions I must make and ponder the guidance I give to my daughters.

Though she died so young, she left a lasting legacy of doing what she thought was right even in the face of opposition, putting others first, standing up for those who had no voice and working toward making the world better for all people. It had a powerful influence on me and I strive to honor that legacy every day.

Gossamer

Memory floats like gossamer strands

On a summer breeze

Visible yet just

Out of reach

Fragments of images

Like memories of dreams

Escaping upon awakening

Into untraceable pathways

One thread of time

Floats just outside awareness

And I try to hold it

To give it form and color

To fully remember

But, like gossamer,

It eludes my grasp

Chapter Four

THE JOURNEY

When I was four months shy of my tenth birthday my youngest sister, Megan, was born. I adored her. I must have learned from my mother how to feed, soothe, diaper and care for a baby, but I don't remember any formal lessons. I just absorbed it from watching her and did all of those things for my sister.

With this being her seventh child, my mom was very experienced and comfortable in her role. I learned mothering from a master. I was at a perfect age to be responsible for my little sister and I remember very clearly lying down with her to get her to take a nap. Megan always wanted to be sure that someone was with her while she slept, so she would have a hand on me as she drifted off to sleep. The tricky part was then trying to slide out from beside her without waking her. I mastered that technique at the ripe old age of eleven.

With that history and my family's large size, I always thought that becoming a mother was just a matter of time and that when my husband and I decided we were ready it would follow as a matter of course. Imagine my surprise when, once I was married and we decided to start a family, months and months passed and we were still not expecting. It was the beginning of a very long journey to motherhood.

Infertility creates an exhausting array of feelings. Emotions run from the high of hopeful waiting to the low of failing, yet again, every single month. We had been trying to get pregnant for two years when I was first placed on a mild fertility drug, and we were thrilled to find ourselves expecting shortly thereafter. My doctor began monitoring my blood levels of beta HCG (an indicator of the growth of the baby) closely. For a few weeks we were filled with joy and excitement.

Grief hit me like a tsunami when the call came and gave us the terrible news that the tests showed I had miscarried.

I sat on the edge of my bed unable to stop crying, absorbing the fullness of our loss, then walked across the hall to what would have been the baby's room. There I saw the one thing I had allowed myself to buy when we first heard we were expecting, a cast iron

Peter Rabbit doorstop. There was Peter in his little blue coat pulling up a carrot from Mr. McGregor's garden. He epitomized the simple joys we had hoped to share with our child and he looked forlorn there in that empty room.

We did not know then how long our journey would be, nor how much grief we would endure before it reached its end. It took two more years of hoping and quiet grieving, month by long month, before I became pregnant again. This time we did not tell anyone, too afraid of the possibility of having to then share sad news if it came again. At eight weeks we lost that child, too. After another devastating wave of sorrow we began the cycle all over; wait, tenuously hope, grieve and wait again.

It was a time of gray skies and great uncertainty as we faced the possibility that we might never have children. Many tears were shed, and Jerry and I held each other up through the failures and the sorrow. After six years, three lost pregnancies, surgeries, shots and tears, I got pregnant again. We kept the news quiet for a long time. Finally, after the first trimester and multiple ultrasounds that showed not one but two babies with normal development and strongly beating hearts, we finally felt able to share our good news with family. I could hardly speak, so full was my heart when we were all gathered to celebrate Megan's birthday and made our announcement. The summer months passed with friends and family throwing showers and sharing our excitement. We were overjoyed when we welcomed our healthy twin girls, Alyssa Ann and Carly Rose, to the world in August of 1996.

Waiting

Unspent joy, simmering within me

waiting to become complete, known

The future beckons with images

long awaited, oft denied

Yet, fearful, I hesitate

to open my mind and heart

to the wholeness of the promise

Will the darkness fall again

taking with it my dreams

I cannot bear to let doubt cloud

my vision of hope

though memory is fresh

of joys lost, dreams denied

I will not let the shadows block out the light

For hope is stronger than fear

and faith takes my hand

guiding me on this path toward the light

Chapter Five

THE STRONGEST BOND

We had a swivel rocking chair placed by our front window when our girls were born. I could rest my arms holding two snuggling babies cuddled close and gently rock the chair with my back and neck comfortably supported. It was my favorite place to hold them. Carly and Alyssa could reach up, touch my face and look into my eyes as I sang and talked to them. We spent many hours there in those early weeks as they often drifted off to sleep in my arms. Those moments are amongst the most treasured of my life.

Rocking my daughters, touching them, singing to them I established bonds that I have learned are vitally important. There is something very primal about the bond a child has with its mother, something powerful and essential. A mother is usually the first "other" of whom a child becomes aware and she remains a touchstone, a reference point, throughout his or her life. She is fundamental to her child's sense of self.

I have learned there is a critical time in a child's life when having that bond is absolutely necessary to healthy development. A child must receive consistent physical affection and attention during this period to fully develop both neurologically and physically. The actual architecture of a child's brain is formed by these interactions. If a child doesn't have this, the connections between neurons that are so vital to thought, behavior and relationship are not made and the child's capacity to learn is impacted for the rest of her life.

That critical time frame is within the first year of life. Children who are denied nurturing care during this period will have significant difficulty creating any attachments to others through their life and are forever scarred by its effects. Receiving mothering from someone in those early months is essential to building relationships through the remainder of life.

Developmental psychologist Urie Bronfenbrenner used these words: ..."in order to develop normally, a child requires... one or more adults who have an irrational emotional relationship with the child.

Somebody's got to be crazy about that kid. That's number one. First, last, and always."

I continue to be awed by the strength of this bond between mother and child. It's the most powerful force that I know. It transcends time and place, and is broken by neither separation nor death. It is the most remarkable connection I have ever experienced. When my mom died, I felt as if I had been set adrift. I was no longer anchored to her, and it was a feeling of aloneness like no other I had ever known. The bond I was not even consciously aware of had been severed and, though I had already begun creating a life separate from my parents, I felt its loss keenly.

Becoming a mother myself deepened my sense of connection with the divine, as the love I've experienced with my daughters is so strong I can't explain it except by looking beyond the human level to a greater power. Everything I've read or heard from other mothers convinces me I am not alone in this. Like great music or art, it touches the emotions, the senses and the intellect in ways that words alone cannot.

Poem For My Mother

I was in you as

my children were in me

and the strength of that bond

is immeasurable

I miss your presence, your laugh,

your powerful love

the things I will never know

I never learned from you

I hold to the knowledge gained

from my own mothering

that your love for me

is not bound by life

by corporeal existence

but transcends all

and will be carried forth

by my children

and theirs

Chapter Six

IT'S ALL IN THE ATTITUDE

When both our baby girls were sick at the same time, I often had nights with almost no sleep at all. I spent hours walking and singing and holding those tiny, hot bodies trying to get them to sleep even for a short time. By morning I was close to tears.

After one of these nights, Jerry came in early the next morning to the girls' room to check on us. I was walking with one of them in my arms when he asked how the night had gone.

"I am so tired." I moaned, "I haven't slept more than a few minutes at a time all night. I don't know how I'm going to make it through the day. I'm just so tired!" He paused and I was waiting for him to console me.

"It's all in the attitude, honey" he said.

Well, my attitude took a decided turn for the worse right then. I do not swear very often, but I swore at him then and said, "Attitude? Attitude?!? You try having a good attitude when you haven't slept for two days!" It shocked him into laughter. Wisely, he retreated from the room, returning a short time later with apologies and concern. After an apology of my own, we resumed the dance that is parenting and made our way through another day.

He was right about choosing to have a good attitude; it does make a huge difference. I just wasn't ready to hear it right then. And so we all learn as we go, we learn how to parent and how to partner and how to laugh at ourselves.

I found the hard work of mothering doesn't end as your children pass out of infancy and into childhood. It just changes. Instead of the constant physical demands of the early months, there was a shift into the need for constant vigilance to prevent injury and guidance and discipline to shape behavior. It continued to be exhausting, just on a different level.

I read once that a typical young child asks around two hundred questions a day. I had two asking at the same time, so I figure four hundred questions a day, seven days a week; we were looking at answering two thousand eight hundred questions each week. No wonder I was weary and my patience wore thin during those early years. There were times when I know I answered with less than a loving tone when, yet again, I heard that question in their voice when they started with "Mama?"

As our children grew, my husband and I had to adapt to new and challenging issues. Peer relationships influenced them more, media had an ever larger role in their lives, school and sports activities occupied much of their energy and they spent less and less time in the sphere of our influence. The challenges of adolescence are those of the mind and heart. Guiding children through these years requires patience, wisdom, and a strong sense of self. It can be exhausting in its own way, as they push against their parents on their way to finding their own path in the world.

Often, they don't understand themselves what they are thinking and feeling. It is a maelstrom of emotion, thoughts, ideas, and doubts all twirling around together. They need love and guidance from someone who can see beyond the prickly exterior to the child that is still learning and growing within. They still need mothering. Children at this stage need to know that they are loved, despite their awkwardness and through their attempts to differentiate themselves from their parents. Somebody still needs to be crazy about that child.

Mothering is hard work, at times. When I think of my mom, who raised seven children, I am in awe of what she accomplished. I never heard her complain, but in hindsight I now understand her occasional sharp words and short temper. It's no wonder that her attitude took a nosedive at times, with the weight of child rearing bearing down on her for so many years.

To My Mother, Twenty Years After Her Death

All those nights you must have spent
waking to every sound
guiding and nurturing each one of us
filling need after need
The drifts of laundry
ever waiting to be done
meals cooked, dishes cleaned
house maintained
the challenges of tedium
the necessities of life
carried heavily in your hands

And we, unknowingly,
taking all you gave
as if it were always to be
with the arrogance of youth
thoughtless and sure
in our perceived immortality

Change is the only constant
we know that now
and nothing will always be

but the love you had for us

fierce and strong

flows through us

and on

and on

Chapter Seven

GOOD MOTHERS

I don't think there is one perfectly right way to mother. I also don't believe that children are completely molded by their parents into who they are. Being the mother of fraternal twins, I had my own small laboratory experiment in the nature/nurture question, and I know that children are who they are right from the beginning.

Alyssa and Carly had an identical prenatal experience, the same parents at the same time with the same cultural exposures, educational experiences and economic situation and yet they're distinctly different from one another. They are two separate individuals, uniquely themselves. Yet, as their mother, I know I was critical in giving these two beautiful souls a start on the path of life. I impacted how they respond to the world, how confident they are in facing obstacles, their sense of self and their expectations of others.

In this media-suffused world in which we live, examples of poor mothering are plentiful. But for every example of poor mothering that comes to the attention of the public, there are multitudes of good mothers that never receive any attention whatsoever. They do this remarkable work of raising children, with all its attendant challenges and difficulties as well as its transcendent joys, and get no recognition. It is mostly taken for granted when it should be celebrated and honored. I believe it's essential to celebrate and support these hard working women.

All kinds of women can be good mothers. We should celebrate and value the variety of women doing the extraordinary job of mothering, in all the myriad ways that they do it. For it is in the ordinary actions of ordinary women that life makes its way: waking in the night to care for a sick child; preparing meals and keeping a clean, healthy home; reading, talking and singing to their children, telling them the stories of life; teaching and supporting their learning; disciplining and providing moral guidance. These incredible women do this every day and every night, looking for no credit, asking for no tribute, just hoping that their children will live good and long lives.

I try to be conscious of promoting and paying tribute to women who are doing this amazing work in my day to day interactions. When I see a young mother in the store and her children are behaving well, I tell her what a good job she is doing. I compliment women on their mothering when I have gotten to know their kids and see what wonderful people they are. It is human nature to thrive on positive feedback. We all love to hear that we're doing something well and mothering may be the most demanding job for which one receives the least positive feedback of any that I know.

You never know how much your words may mean to a mother in the midst of raising children. It is usually a very thankless job. We don't get performance appraisals from our kids and, if we did, we probably would never get a raise as their perspective is skewed as to what constitutes doing the job well. So give those moms around you a word of praise, acknowledge their work and be free with your compliments. Who else understands better than other mothers how difficult it can be? Acknowledgement from you of their efforts could change their whole perspective and give them strength when they need it.

I remember asking my mother, when I'd reached an age where I started to comprehend how difficult raising children was, how she had managed to do it; how had she handled having four children with the oldest being just four when the latest (me) was born? Her answer to me then encapsulated the wisdom of women through the ages, "You just take one day at a time and do what needs to be done."

Women have been doing what needs to be done for thousands upon thousands of years. Today we have the benefit of medical advances, education, access to information, disposable diapers, microwave ovens, washing machines and, still, we find it difficult to raise our children. It is amazing to me to think about how women did it before the conveniences of modern life were available. It's really a miracle that I'm even here, that all my ancestors survived and then had children that survived. I'm deeply indebted to them for the difficulties and hard work they must've endured in order for their descendants to flourish. I am fortunate that they were good mothers.

Gratitude

That I live at all is a tribute

to all of you,

Mothers and grandmothers

of ages past

Your toil and trouble

Your love and sacrifice

The glory of your lives

I know not your names or faces

Your stories or your sorrows

Yet I am of you and with you

I carry your legacy onward

in the world

And I am grateful

Chapter Eight

CONNECTIONS

I was the fourth child in a family of seven and my mom was busy during my early years. I don't have a baby book. She made one for my oldest sister, started one for the second child, bought one for the third but did not write much in it, and didn't even attempt one for me. There is no record of how old I was when I took my first steps, what my first word was or even when I got my first tooth. I have only a few undated black and white pictures over the course of those first few years, and no keepsakes or locks of hair. My dad doesn't remember those things, so my early childhood is mostly an unknown to me.

When my daughters were born I decided to be very disciplined in writing down milestones and in placing pictures with at least a little written about them into baby books and photo albums. I was determined that whether I was present or not, those images and facts would be there for them when they were old enough to wonder about their past. I wanted them to have that knowledge, to feel connected to their own childhoods and to be able to pass some of their stories on to the next generation. Once I had children of my own, I wondered about my early development and felt keenly the gaps in my knowledge of my own history. I wanted our girls to have a written record of theirs, so it could never be lost.

Mothers are often the ones who link their children to the past. As the living tie to their ancestors, we are the bearers of memory and experience. We tell our children the stories of their own lives and the stories of their families. It is an important task, keeping that history alive. All of us are part of many stories, some of which we know well and others of which we may be completely unaware. If I don't tell my children their stories, they won't be able to pass them on to their children, and much of the richness of that heritage will be lost.

Children are also our link to the future, a means of connecting to generations yet to come. They are our legacy. There are many other ways that women can leave a legacy, yet this world would not continue to exist were it not for women bearing, loving and successfully raising their children. We mold in our hands the clay upon which the future is built. It all comes down to love, really. Mothers tell stories, keep baby books and photos and care for our children because we love them. For mothering is, at its heart, about love.

As a mother, I am like a spider creating a web of connection between past and future, casting out strands in many directions and knitting them all together, creating a lovely weaving of history and possibility.

The Love of a Mother

It cannot be bought or sold or broken

It is a force fierce and unequaled

Spanning lifetimes and crossing oceans

Carrying within it the power of God

It protects and challenges, nurtures and guides

Following its bearers all the days of their lives

Borne in the deepest part of their hearts

A balm against the ills of the world

It is the genesis of life

The source of unending strength

As it passes from one to another

It is hope and joy, faith and trust

It is the love of a mother

Chapter Nine

HAVING ENOUGH

After my daughters were born, I did not go back to work for several years. We chose to give up my income so that I could be their fulltime caregiver. That decision made some things easier and some harder. It was easier because we didn't have to worry if one of the girls got sick, I could adjust to their schedules and didn't have to force them into keeping ours, and they had my constant, mostly undivided attention. That was a gift both to them and to me. At the same time, the financial burden created some difficulties. We used up some of our savings during those years and lived as frugally as we could. Jerry bore the heavy weight of financially supporting all of us.

What does it mean to have it all? I ponder that question every time I read an article about women and their decisions regarding balancing mothering with work outside the home. That has become the catch phrase for characterizing women who want to do both. Most of us don't want to have it all, we just want to have enough. What is essential is that the personal needs of the children are met, while the financial needs of the family are met, as well.

When the girls were four years old, I took a position working weekends in a hospital physical therapy department. This took some of the financial pressure off but limited our time together as a family as every day one parent was working. Once they started school, I began working as much as I could as an on-call physical therapist during school hours. This allowed me to be home when the girls were, and we didn't have to pay for any childcare outside of school hours. The income was variable, but the flexibility was invaluable. We had made it our priority that I was home with them, and we made it work. I feel very lucky to have had that option.

The fact is that most women with children do work outside the home in some fashion, and must make arrangements for child care. Women have been balancing work and caring for their children as long as there have been humans. In the past, more closely entwined family groups made it easier to build a caregiving network. Today, the challenge is that extended family can't always meet that need. Women often live far from their relatives and must find another way. They hire caregivers, work alternate schedules with their partner or send their children to daycare. The bottom line is that women can't do it alone.

The most important factor in this equation is the quality of the care that the children receive. If they are well nurtured, they will thrive. Today's children become the adults of tomorrow, and caring for them during the critical time when their minds and bodies are developing is our investment in the future. More attention is being paid to this issue, and many different people are striving to create and sustain affordable nurturing environments for children who require care while their parents work. When all children have access to quality care and their parents have jobs that pay enough to support them then we really would have it all.

Enough

As I am aware I cannot have it all

I must decide for me

What is essential?

What's within reach?

What can I do without?

It's the balance that is so hard to find

The fact that we don't know for sure

What lies ahead

On this crooked path

What does our story hold?

At the end of the day I want to have done

My best, to have few regrets

To have known hope and laughter

Shared meaningful days

Given joy to those that I love

To know that the work of my hands and mind

Has lightened the days of a few

To have had a good plenty

Of just enough

Of the pleasures of being alive

For while time is finite

And change ever near

We are given a choice

In how we spend our life, our breath

And that is enough for me

Chapter Ten

A MOTHER'S IMAGE

When I think of a mother, I picture my own. She was not very tall, at only 5'1", but she seemed invincible to me. She had a loud laugh and a beautiful singing voice, and it felt as if she could do just about anything well. Mom kept her dark hair short and her face unadorned by any makeup. She had a natural beauty set off by her clear eyes and big smile. She looked and acted nothing like the mothers I saw on TV or in the movies. But hers was the far more powerful influence on me, and it is to her that I compare myself as a mother. She framed my image of what a mother should be. I realize as I write this that I am doing the same for my own daughters. With all my flaws and strengths, I am their guide to mothering.

My mom could also be quick to anger and sharp of tongue. She did not tolerate talking back and she occasionally reached the limits of her patience. We realized this when either the offending child was sent to their room or, on rare occasions, when whatever object was in her hand was sent in their direction.

One day Mom was standing in our small kitchen, at the stove, cooking dinner. She was wearing a sleeveless, collared shirt and shorts. Her arms were deeply tanned from hours spent sitting in the sun cheering for her kids at swim meets. My older brother, Tim, was in the doorway. He was about twelve years old at the time and I don't remember exactly what he said, but I knew he'd gone too far as soon as the words were out of his mouth. I tensed as Mom spun around and whipped her spatula at him. She didn't say a word. He ducked, it hit the wall where he had been standing, and he wisely left the room quickly. Nothing more was said, she returned to her task and all of us kids were extra quiet as dinner was completed and served. We tread softly that evening, an unspoken agreement between us not to aggravate her any more.

She had probably just finished stripping layers of paint off our front door, or folding flyers and stuffing envelopes for one of her many causes. Mom was dedicated to many things, not least to raising us to be good people. She encouraged each of us to be our best at whatever we were passionate about. She expected us to work hard and show respect. And she didn't put up with bad attitudes.

Mom made us face difficult challenges head on. She let us struggle through them but supported us, as well. My oldest sister, Nora, has told me about a pivotal moment in her childhood. She was taking swimming lessons and she knew that it was her time to dive into the deep-end that day. She was terrified and did not want to go to the pool. She even locked herself in the one place in our house that had a lock on the door, the upstairs bathroom. It didn't work. Mom forced her to go and face her fear. She did dive into the pool that day, and she discovered she was good at it. By the time she was in high school, she was a competitive diver and held the school record for the highest diving score there for many years. She went on to dive in college, as well. Perhaps all of this success could be traced to the day her mom didn't let her give in to her fear.

Mary the Mother

There is a portrait of Mary
on the wall by the door
I see it every day
She holds a cloth in her hands
and a basket lies near her
as if she were just in the middle
of the wash
She is, after all, a mother
with the work of a household to do
for even Jesus required the care
of a mother to live in this world
And a glow is implied by the artist
around and about her head
sanctifying this most ordinary task
the washing of clothes by the mother of God
I like having her in my kitchen
blessing the days of our lives
Her serenity and her knowing smile
remind me that I am not alone
women have done this for thousands of years
and I am a mother, like her

Chapter Eleven

THE FIRST TEACHER

I was my daughters' first teacher. My voice singing lullabies to them, my hand caressing their faces, my smile in response to theirs initiated connections between the very neurons in their brains, beginning the process of memory and knowledge, creating understanding and shaping behavior.

From the time Alyssa and Carly were very small, books were part of our world. I read to them, they held and sometimes chewed on their board books and the books, themselves, became treasured possessions. By the time they were two years old, they were turning the pages and saying the words they had heard so many times. They had their favorites, such as "Brown Bear, Brown Bear" by Eric Carle and "The Big Red Barn" by Margaret Wise Brown, and we read them over and over again, so often we all could recite them by heart. Each time those words became more ingrained into their understanding, and the rhythms and rhymes laid down patterns in their memories. Reading aloud introduced them to new words and concepts.

We also sang many songs together, from "I've Been Working on the Railroad" to the Beatles' "Yellow Submarine" and "Little Boy Blue" to songs from Disney's "The Lion King" and "The Jungle Book" movies. The power of words shared, songs sung and the lovely patterns of language and music all contributed to their ability to communicate with and understand others as they continued their education.

Teachers and schools are integral in the education of our children, and the work they do is vitally important. A good connection between teachers and parents is what creates the optimal environment for a child to excel. But we mothers are our child's first teacher. We have the power to frame our child's view of learning and to give them a strong start in life by making it a joyful and engaging thing.

Lessons

From you I learn to take my cues
Through the vagaries of life
Is this a time for laughter
Is it OK to cry
Should I mostly trust
Or fear
Can I wander safely
Or rather keep you near
Shall I take the easy way
Or risk the hard
Knowing I might fail
Is it good to puzzle over ideas
And struggle to understand
Do I fear the stranger over there
Or extend a helping hand
Lessons absorbed
Whether known or not
As I stand at your knee
For you are my anchor
And my moor
From you will I set sail
Into the uncertain winds
Of life

Chapter Twelve

BEING STILL

When our girls were small, my husband was wonderful at recognizing when my energy tank was getting close to empty, and he would encourage me to take a little time to myself. He often knew before I did that I was running low on "soul food," and it was a great gift to have his support and encouragement to replenish my self. His thoughtfulness and concern for me during those early years of motherhood solidified my gratitude for his perceptive and loving presence in my life. I was lucky that he saw the importance of feeding the soul.

Feeding the soul is as important to life as feeding the body. It's not easy to do with the insistent demands on our time from all the competing roles we fill. It's very difficult to achieve balance among them while still sustaining the core of self. We commonly set aside time for exercise, but few of us make time just to be alone. We are so inculcated in the idea that we must be "doing something" that we don't allow ourselves to do nothing. Yet, in doing nothing, we allow ourselves time to feed our soul, to nurture our inner self, to contemplate and to breathe. "Be still and know that I am God" says the scripture. It is the "be still" part that so many of us have trouble doing.

Jerry created a space for us in our own backyard that has become our spot for being still. It's our Zen place, and I retreat to it often. The sound of running water from the small waterfall he built fills the air, and the water cascading over stones soothes and calms me. A simple roof overhead, supported by columns clad with cedar and stone protects from the elements, but does not remove us from them. There I sit and am still, watching the birds or the trees in the wind. There we ground ourselves and renew our connection to the earth. It's a holy place. We have made it so by choosing to be still there.

In 1955, Anne Morrow Lindbergh wrote a small book called "Gift from the Sea". I love this book. It resonated with me as I read it during the busy years of my girls' childhood. It is a beautiful, lyrical meditation on one woman's life in the middle of the last century in the middle of motherhood and marriage. In it she captures many of the challenges facing women through the ages, one of which is how to nurture and sustain the self in the midst of the demands of one's children and spouse. She wrote it while taking a rare sojourn to the beach, alone.

It's as true now as it was then, that women are pulled in many directions, and she, too, found it difficult to make time and space for the self. As the mother of five children, her life at home was full to the brim with responsibility and activity. On an island beach, alone, she found the time to contemplate and write about the inner life, the self, and the relationship of one woman to her life, her spouse, her children and the world. "The problem," she wrote, "is not entirely in finding the room of one's own, the time alone, difficult and necessary as this is. The problem is more how to still the soul in the midst of its activities. In fact, the problem is how to feed the soul." I have found that taking the time to still my soul helps me be a calmer and, hopefully, a better mother.

Silent Truth

Sound surrounds us

Pervading our lives

Traffic, music, television

Cell phone rings and conversation

How rare and treasured

Is the silence

An absence of

Cacophony

Freeing the mind to wander

The soul to ponder

Refreshing the innermost

Pool of our selves

Life passes so quickly

Be silent and aware

Quiet brings clarity

Making space for truth

Chapter Thirteen

A WONDERFUL GRACE

When I was pregnant with our daughters, I was attuned to the smallest sensations within me. I remember sitting still and trying to sense their movements, wondering what they were able to perceive. I talked and sang to them, and sent loving thoughts, hoping they would absorb it all and thrive. Being able to sense them move inside me, placing my hand on my own stomach and feeling a tiny heel pressing into it or a small bottom shifting around gave me a deep thrill. I shall never again experience the quickening of life inside me, but I'll never forget the profound awe of knowing that I had two separate souls within my body and that I was part of such a miraculous process as creating new life.

Just to be able to perceive the world around me, to ponder things, to listen to music, to feel love is an incredible gift. If I were to die tomorrow, my life would be complete. I've known moments of exquisite beauty, deep sadness and profound joy and have had the love of a wonderful man and two beautiful and gracious daughters. I've had a supportive and caring family and have seen goodness and kindness in many whose paths have crossed mine. I have been lifted by music, surrounded by prayer, and held in great love. Who could ask for more than that?

I want our girls to know this: life is a gift. I don't want them going through their lives "unconscious" as the German spiritual teacher Eckhart Tolle calls it. His teaching states the ego or the voice that is the stream of involuntary thinking and emotion most of us pay attention to is not our true self. It's when we are aware of that voice that our true self is present and we are fully conscious.

We are the awareness that lies behind the voice, and that awareness allows us to be in touch with the oneness of all life. Taking this attitude has made everything richer for me. In being grateful for and in touch with even the smallest things, a gentle rain, the slow flow of an old river, bird songs in the morning, life becomes full of wonder and joy.

As a mother, I feel deeply the joy of having given that gift of life to my daughters. I provided sustenance as they grew within me. I delivered them safely to the world and I nurtured them as they grew. What an incredible grace to be the bearer of such wonder! It's the most rewarding thing I've ever done.

Thin Places

The minister talks about thin places

Those times when it seems we can reach out and touch divinity

When the distance between here

and there Is lessened and

the view is unobscured

And our most inner selves

are opened

I find them often

when I am not looking

in the soft warmth of a small body

tucked into the curve of my arm

when a sweet swell of beautiful music

carries me away

in the quiet of an ordinary morning,

cup of coffee in hand,

watching the day begin

in the still of night with my husband beside me,

held fast by his love and grace

I find them, too,

when I am ready to receive them

in the speaking of our wedding vows

seeing the breathtaking beauty

of two newborn girls

watching those now-grown girls

sing reverently in the choir

at the front of the church

As I grow older, the thin places seem

easier to reach

Or maybe I am just opening up

To the divinity

that has always been here

Chapter Fourteen

SPREADING KINDNESS

For many years as Carly and Alyssa were growing up, we participated in our church's Christmas tradition of adopting families and buying presents based on their wish lists. These families were linked to our church through social service agencies or schools in the area, and many of their wishes were for basic necessities of life like laundry baskets and winter coats. I made a point of having the girls help with the shopping, and they got to choose one special thing as an extra gift for each child in our Christmas family.

As they grew older, they joined the church's high school youth group which would adopt families at Christmas too, and they went shopping together with donated funds. I chaperoned this excursion one year. There was a new member of the youth group that year, a young man with autism. I watched as my daughters took the time to make him feel part of the group and even gave him one of their Santa hats to wear through the store as they shopped. Their kindness to him as they participated in this tradition of giving epitomized the joy of the season.

The Dalai Lama said, "Be kind whenever possible....It is always possible." In every interaction between two people, there are a multitude of possible behaviors. We have a choice as to what response to make. We shape our children from the very beginning of their lives by modeling these interactions with others and with them. Showing kindness creates an atmosphere of goodwill. We all fail to be kind at times, of course. No one is perfect. However, if we show kindness to our children, they will learn to be kind.   There used to be commercials on TV that showed this passing on of kindness from one person to another. The thing I like about those commercials is that they are all ordinary acts during an ordinary day; holding the door for someone whose arms are full, letting a harried young mother go ahead in the grocery line, stopping a child from going into the street. They are simple things and only require a little thoughtfulness. Mother Teresa said "We cannot do great things, only small things with great love." It is the small things we do for others in a spirit of kindness that makes life enjoyable.

I believe being kind is a conscious choice everyone can make. It's not hard, doesn't require any training, and doesn't cost a thing. It's a way of being, a focus on making others' lives more pleasant. In making this choice, the quality of life of everyone involved is improved. It becomes a self-perpetuating action. I want my daughters' lives to be as joyful as possible and their actions will determine that. I hope they have learned to be kind whenever possible.

Golden

"Be kind." I said as they got out

of the car

To enter the halls of their

middle school

What was left unsaid was all the rest

The knowing of the sorrows

And difficulties of adolescence

The hoping for compassion

on all fronts

That others would also be kind

In their living of that day

"Do unto others"

says the wise woman

And she knows the power therein

The capacity to lift one's own life

Into joy

With the speaking of a gentle word

The sharing of a small moment

of magnanimity

May they learn to listen and care

Look outside themselves

and walk a mile

In another's shoes

For there is a good reason

the Rule is called Golden

Shining like the sun

Shedding light and warmth

into a cold world

"Be kind." I say

And mean so much more

Chapter Fifteen

RITUALS

Some of my earliest memories are of being in church with my family. My family was Catholic, and we attended Mass every Sunday no matter where we were or what was scheduled. Mass was the same every week, and I could speak the words and understand the flow long before I could read. The ritual of it, the traditions of the words spoken, the music sung and the motions of the service were comforting and familiar. I gauged my growth by the pews. I was excited when I was finally able to kneel on the kneeler and see over the top of the pew in front of me with my arms resting on it, hands folded in prayer. It was a sign that I was growing up.

Church was a place of connection, of peace and of learning about my place in the larger world. Children thrive on tradition, on known and loved rituals and words. The prayers of my childhood still bring me peace today.

Though I did not continue to practice the faith of my childhood, its resonance in my life is unmistakable. Because of the strong connection to the divine I had experienced, I wanted to establish a church home for our girls as they grew up. We searched for a while, attending several different denominations of Christianity, before finding one that was a good fit for both my husband and me. We found that the combination of traditional music and rituals combined with a progressive theology made us feel at home. I cannot say that our daughters attended church every Sunday the way I did as a child, but they had a steady commitment to their church which culminated in it being a major influence in their lives by the time they reached high school.

I began a ritual of my own with our girls at night before bed when they were very small. Each of them would choose a lullaby and a prayer and we would sing and say them together. We had a repertoire of perhaps four lullabies and four different prayers, and initially they would rotate them. By the time they were four or five years old, however, each had settled on one lullaby and one prayer that they wanted each and every night. I sang "All the Pretty Ponies" and "Tura Lura Lura" and recited The Lord's Prayer and the Hail Mary with them thousands of times through their childhood years. The sharing of those moments before bed became some of our most treasured times. I hope that those prayers will always be a source of solace to them.

How many people look to the values they learned as a child in determining their path as an adult? Most of us do, if we are honest. Mothers are one of the defining forces in the moral outlook of our children. It is from us that children learn it is important to care for others, to make our homes and communities better, to work for the benefit of the greater good.

I have an innate appreciation of a greater power having been raised in faith and participating in the creation and nurturing of two human souls. My faith and the connection I feel to that divine power continue to grow stronger as I live each day keeping my own rituals and feeling the rhythms of life.

Prayer

There is a comfort in the words
Spoken so often, known and beloved
Cadences roll smoothly off the tongue
Rhythmic and familiar
Connecting us to each other
And to deeper levels of ourselves
Where awareness and instinct meet
And thought goes beyond words
There we join
With countless other souls
In peace and synchronicity
As we make our way
Through this life

Chapter Sixteen

LETTING GO

My daughters have left home and I miss them. I miss hearing them sing "Beauty and the Beast" in the shower, laugh over a shared joke and talk about their friends. I find myself crying at unexpected times. Driving in my car as I listen to the radio, a fragment of a song we sang together can bring me to tears. In the grocery store I see mothers with their children in the cart, and I tear up knowing that will never be me again. I'm in mourning.

I loved having children at home, loved being their mother and sharing their joys and sorrows. It's a strange thing that the goal for which we work so hard creates such emptiness in our lives. I want my girls to be strong, independent people. I just didn't realize how hard it would be to let them go. All my instincts tell me to keep protecting them, teaching them, yet I know I must step back now. It is time for them to apply all the life lessons they have learned on their own. Instead of holding them close, I now must learn how to mother at a distance.

In a way, we begin letting our children go from the moment they're born. When they're growing in the womb, they are completely enveloped by us, safe within our body. Once they're no longer carried inside us, they become separate entities experiencing the world from unique perspectives. We can no longer completely protect them, and times spent apart start to lengthen. When they start day care or preschool we have to let them go a little more, giving up direct responsibility to trusted others who guide and care for them for part of the day.

Through their school years they grow even more independent, stretching those hours when they are outside our circle of care. We gradually learn how to let them go through all these stages, always keeping the lines of connection intact, the path back to us clear. Though it's almost imperceptible, they gain autonomy and separate themselves from us more and more with the passage of time. When they move away from home, however, it is a stark and sudden change. It brings into clear focus that these are no longer children, they are now adults. I don't really know how to mother an adult, yet. I am just starting on that journey.

So Close

So close, so close

Beneath my heart

Kept safe and warm and near

My child you grew and came to be

Miraculous and dear

Then close I held you in my arms

Rocked and sang and talked

Smiling at you, eyes and heart

First you crawled

Then walked

A little further from me then

You ventured

Climbed and twirled

Two driveways to the

right and left

Then out into the world

Slowly I've been letting go

A gradual release

Trusting, hoping

Praying, too

That you would find your peace

Though miles now

Between us lie

And life draws us apart

So close I hold you still, my child

Deep within my heart

Chapter Seventeen

LOVE AND LOSS

When my mom underwent a bone marrow transplant for her cancer, it was still an experimental treatment and she had to stay in a hospital in Omaha, Nebraska to be part of a study. My family lived in Des Moines, Iowa, two hours east, and I was in school at the University of Iowa in Iowa City, a further two hours east. I felt very far away from her.

She had been in the hospital for a few weeks and it was almost Mother's Day. I had always just given Mom a card with a carefully written message for Mother's Day in years past. We were not a demonstrative family. Birthdays were acknowledged with a card and cake, parties were not expected, and holidays were occasions to gather for a meal. This year I wanted to do more. Ordering flowers seemed to be a perfect way to show her that I loved her extravagantly, so I called a florist in Omaha and ordered a dozen red roses to be delivered to her hospital room with my heartfelt message of love.

Expensive and unexpected, I hoped they would show her how much I cared.

The day before Mother's Day, I received a call from the florist that they were not able to deliver the flowers to my mom as she was in an isolation room. Her immune system was so suppressed they could not allow any possibility of infection, so the flowers could not be in her room. She never even got to see them. I was devastated and cried for a long time. I grieved because I realized then I would never be able to fully show my mom how much I loved her. Mom died less than a month later. I never got to send her flowers.

It is inevitable when one loves deeply that there will be loss. They are two sides of the same coin; one cannot exist without the other. I believe it is only through love that we can heal after a great loss. And without love, life is empty. The love of my family, my husband and eventually my daughters all helped my heart heal over the years from the crushing loss of my mom after her death.

The Path

Death and Birth

Loss and Joy

Love and Grief

Inexorably entwined

Neither one without

The other

And we in our living

Tread softly

The unmarked path between

Chapter Eighteen

THE MIRACLE OF LIFE

It was miraculous and even a little frightening to witness the changes that occurred in my body during pregnancy. With no conscious effort, intricate processes within my very cells combined to result in the perfect environment for a growing baby. I was awed by my body's ability to alter itself and the powerful emotions that swept over me. On a deep and instinctive level, I felt the great life force.

The first time I saw those two little hearts beating on the ultrasound monitor was a profound moment. It made distinctly clear that within my body lived two separate and unique beings. Millions of women experience this, but before I was one of them, I didn't truly understand the power of that process, the incredible miracle of life. To realize that I couldn't control the outcome, yet bore the responsibility of nourishing and caring for these children was humbling. I felt the power of the life force within me.

I'm continually amazed by the spectacular diversity and persistence of life on this earth. Life always finds a way to exist. Everywhere you look, life is trying to renew itself. Plants scatter their seeds, birds make nests and lay their eggs, roots dive deep into the earth and human beings have children. In the face of challenges, harsh conditions or scarcity of resources, life persists and thrives. It has a remarkable ability to adapt and shows fantastic resilience as new stresses and demands are placed upon it.

What is this force that creates life? Why is there such a powerful drive to renew and continue it? I believe that there's a divine power and that all the miraculous processes that we are the beneficiaries of are part of its creation. I am fascinated by life's processes: the intricacy of the human brain, the adaptability of tissue, the capacity we have to heal, the incredible process of reproduction. I believe the study of these is an important part of our obligation to nurture and sustain life on this earth.

But what is most intriguing to me is the question of why. Why are we here? Why does life exist at all? Those are questions that I ponder. Yet I am content to leave them unsolved. I believe that it's enough to exist and to perceive and to think. How I choose to be and what I choose to do are the only things I really control. I choose to love and to nurture life and to try my best to add positive energy to this world. That's my choice. That's how I want to live this gift of life I've been given.

Tiny Miracles

When they were tiny

I marveled

at all the perfectly

formed parts

beautiful and miraculous

how could such intricacy

come to be

proteins and atoms

elements of creation

forming a unique

creative, loving

soul

with thought, language

and the capacity

to marvel

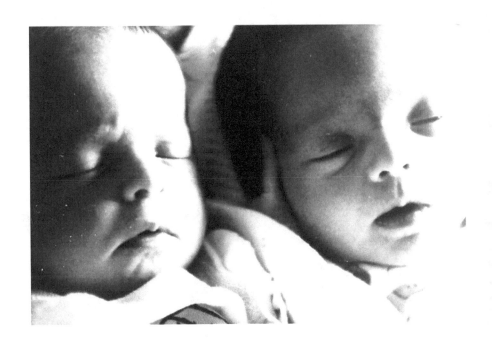

Chapter Nineteen

FATHERS

As a child during the 1960's and 1970's, I didn't realize just how special my dad was. He was a young attorney in a large law firm, and he had a lot of demands placed upon him by his colleagues and partners. Yet I knew nothing of that. He had a beat up old leather briefcase which was always stuffed with papers that he would bring home every night. As far as I knew, he never picked it up again until he left the next morning for work. Once home, he was focused on his children and his family.

I remember playing Around the World and countless games of PIG at the basketball hoop above the door of our garage. Dad had a killer hook shot that I had a hard time making, so he usually won. He attended every athletic, music or theater event in which any of his children was involved. He played with us, challenged us and raced us across the front yard (until my oldest sister could beat him). In short, he was a great father.

My dad, Donald J. Brown, was the youngest of a family of eight children from a farm family in northwest Iowa. He was born in the midst of the Dust Bowl years. There were nine years between him and his next oldest sibling, so he spent a lot of time alone wandering the fields during his childhood. He developed a great love of the outdoors, especially of its bird life, and this became a lifelong passion.

As a child, I had trading cards not of baseball players but of birds and animals. We would memorize them and compete to see who knew the most when Dad would flash them to us. His love of birds drove many of our vacation destinations, too, as he was trying to add to his life list of birds seen. We grew up enjoying exploring the outdoors and valuing its beauty and diversity.

My husband is a thoughtful and involved father, as well. He has a gift for making up games using whatever is at hand and many of these games have become treasured memories for our girls and their cousins. He transformed himself into a very lovable monster that hid three items and "chased" the kids until they found them all, at which point they were safe. He pitched thousands of balls not only to our girls but to the other kids in our neighborhood who gathered for games of backyard baseball. He untangled fishing lines and put worms on hooks for our girls and their cousins for hours at a time. He told stories and watched for falling stars with them. He showed them how a good man loves his family.

I met my husband, Jerry W. Hewitt, Jr., when I was a freshman at the University of Iowa. He was a sophomore and we met in tennis class. He made me laugh. I watched how he joked with others in the class, with no ego and no attitude. Always gentle, willing to make himself the target of the laughter, he was also talented and athletic. We began walking back to the dorms together after class and saw each other in the cafeteria. Friends first, the romance had time to develop gradually.

We began dating after a few months and it was clear to me then that this was a special man. He was with me through my mother's illness and death and was my biggest support during that time. We developed a very strong bond that continued to grow and deepen through the years, and we got married after over five years of dating, after college and graduate school. Many years have passed since those early days and we continue to laugh and grow together. I chose wisely.

I'm lucky to have him in my life and blessed to have him father my children. With deep humility I recognize that I, alone, couldn't have raised these girls as well as they've been raised with both of us parenting. They gain from each of us separate but complementary things. Fathering is as critical as mothering when the outcome of whole, healthy and loving children is the goal. I've been fortunate to have had a great father and to have married a great father.

Our Atlas

Countless times you carried them
Shoulder rides around the house
"Again, daddy, again"
They cried with glee
Swept up in joy
Thrilled with the speed
Confident of their safety
In your arms

Through you they learned
That the world is magical
Games are most fun
When everyone wins
That love is strong and gentle
And making people laugh
Is a wonderful thing

You gave us all our daily bread
Along with so very much more
For like Atlas you carried our world
Supporting and nurturing
Through the wind and rain
And we are forever grateful
For your strong shoulders

Chapter Twenty

WHAT MATTERS MOST

On the bulletin board by my desk in the kitchen, I have posted the words from Hebrews 13:2 "Be not forgetful to entertain strangers for thereby some have entertained angels unawares." I keep it there to remind myself that anyone at any time may be a messenger from God.

When I was in the middle of the waiting, the uncertainty and the sorrow associated with our struggles to get pregnant, I was teaching part of my day in a program for students working on their Masters in Physical Therapy degree. I didn't know the students well and had not shared any of my personal life with them. One day a young woman came to me in class and said, "I had such a clear dream about you last night. I dreamed you had twins and you were showing them to the class. I think they were boys and one was named Nathaniel." I never got to tell her the good news that I did, in fact, eventually have twins, though they were girls and neither was named Nathaniel. She was an angel to me then, a messenger bearing tidings of great joy, for her dream gave me hope. She probably doesn't know how much it meant to me that she shared her dream with me that day.

I believe divinity resides in everyone and all of us are made in the image of God. At any given time we may be angels to one another. We play a part in many lives: creating connections, sowing ideas, sharing compassion, bestowing a smile. As mothers, we do that for our children, but we can also be angels to many others along the way.

Life is a puzzle at times, an intricate interplay of patterns and chaos. We don't know what will come next or whether our plans will come to fruition. It can feel as if we are walking a constantly shifting path, never quite certain of our destination. Sometimes we are filled with joy, at times blindsided by grief. It's a continuously changing landscape, like a kaleidoscope turning from one combination of colors and shapes to another.

Life changes constantly, varying from joy to sorrow, ordinary to spectacular in turns. Its meaning evolves through the stages and experiences of each of us. What is important in this living? On what should we spend our attention and time? The relationships we build with others are the essence of a meaningful life, for it's in these relationships that we experience love. As human beings, with divinity residing within us, I believe love is our highest calling, and as a mother, love for my children is the greatest gift I can give the world. They will continue to pass on that gift, and it will thrive long after I am gone as it passes from them and on out into the world.

My mother kept a saying posted in her kitchen, too. Many years after she died, I carefully wrote the words in calligraphy and it's now framed and displayed in my home.

Prayer from Cardinal Newman

God has created me
to do Him some definite service.
He has committed some work to me which He
has not committed to another.
I HAVE MY MISSION
I may never know it in this life,
but I shall be told it in the next.
I AM A LINK IN A CHAIN
A bond of connection between persons.

He has not created me for naught.

I shall do good – I shall do His work.

I shall be an angel of peace, a preacher of truth in my own place

while not intending it if I do but keep His commandments.

THEREFORE WILL I TRUST HIM

Whatever I am, I can never

be thrown away.

If I am in sickness, my sickness may serve Him, in perplexity,

my perplexity may serve Him.

If I am in sorrow,

my sorrow may serve Him.

HE DOES NOTHING IN VAIN

He knows what He is about.

He may take away my friends,

He may throw me among strangers.

He may make me feel desolate,

make my spirits sink,

hide my future from me – still

He knows what he is about.

This took on new poignancy after her death. I came to appreciate the depth and beauty of the message more as my life progressed. I thank her for this, and for all I learned from her and from her life.

Ponder and live a meaningful life. Nurture your relationships with others. Be kind. Treasure your mothering and know its worth. The world owes you its thanks.

Angels Among Us

Walking among us in many guises

These quiet messengers carry their grace

Unnoticed at times

Asking the hard questions

Leaving hope and blessings in their wake

Mothers and friends, strangers and teachers

Fellow travelers on this fascinating journey

Unknowing angels bearing invisible feathers

As they touch us with their light